GAME CHANGER

**Understanding the Key to
Improved Results
in Sales and in Life.**

Kyle Dietrich

GREEN IVY
PUBLISHING

Green Ivy Publishing
1 Lincoln Centre
18W140 Butterfield Road
Suite 1500
Oakbrook Terrace IL 60181-4843
www.greenivybooks.com

Game Changer/Kyle Dietrich

ISBN: 978-1-946775-89-4
Ebook: 978-1-946775-90-0

Faith and trust in the "all of it," and the continued quest for appreciation of the present moment.   Thank you for that Pamela. Game Changer just wouldn't be the same without you.   **<3 <3 <3**

Game Changer

Understanding the Key to Improved Results in Sales and in Life

Quotes:

Do you believe that the key to success and happiness exists out in the world, but you have been unable to find it? "Game Changer" will teach you that the silver bullet you crave is not an external force, but an internal passion that is waiting to be ignited. This book will give you valuable techniques and an organized game plan to change your mindset and unlock your potential to build a successful, balanced life. While the concepts in this book are focused on building a successful sales career, anyone looking to make a change or improvement in their life will find value in "Game Changers". Success is simple, but not easy!

David Coe

Owner of The COE Real Estate Team and For Investors, By Investors.

What I love about *Game Changer* is that it is so refreshingly unassuming and real. What separates this book from others in its genre are Dietrich's highly unique perspectives, which breathe new life and excitement into an overly analyzed topic. In the short hour it takes to read, *Game Changer* offers extraordinary bang for the buck, and provides a clear road map not only to success in sales, but to success in life. This book will resonate deeply with anyone who has both the desire and discipline to step up their game.

Mike Wunderli

Wharton School of Business MBA; CEO Connect Capital Group; Managing Director of ECHELON Partners.

Contents

Introduction

Introduction

If you are reading this book, or may have just picked it up to determine if there is value inside, you are already one of millions who put forth the effort to seek improvement: improvement in their results, improvement in themselves, and improvement in life in general.

Being a sales and sales leadership professional, I too have read many publications with the intent of learning, improving, seeking that next rung on the ladder, whether it is professionally or financially inclined. So why this book? Why does the content within the confines of this book cover matter to you? Why do these words of wisdom carry weight, and how can they truly benefit you?

From a results perspective, I come from twenty-three–plus years of executing in a sales capacity both individually and extensively in sales leadership roles. In thirteen years as a vice president of sales for three different entities, I have faced down the most difficult of clients and tackled the most challenging of goals. I've been kicked out of offices, been told my company is a joke

Introduction

and that I should find a real job, and overcome all those scenarios to drive success. I've sat elbow to elbow with stiff competition and pressed forward with consistent results that exceeded objectives time and time again. In building successful sales organizations, I have hired hundreds, coached people to success, and watched many fall by the wayside.

In the process of overcoming the challenges and facing the objections of an industry pitch for pitch, account by account, and success story over success story, I began to find a clear pattern for success that revealed itself through the building of successful sales teams and individuals. To find sustained success, we need to face our own fears and completely understand our role in our results.

In your development, it is important to feel the sting of failure and discover the powerful motivational tool these experiences can give you. I have talked the talk, and I have walked the walk and, in doing so, have helped create a myriad of highly -compensated sales professionals.

Introduction

In this book, I can share with you the common themes that become apparent in those individuals who separated themselves from the pack, and earned a healthy income in the process.

On a personal level, I've overcome cancer, I'm a full-time single dad, and I have met and overcame the challenge of a sudden career change in the most challenging of economies. My message to you is simple: I have overcome great challenges in life, and I have built high-performing success stories in both individuals and sales teams, and you can benefit from these experiences.

In this book, I will share with you where the true catalyst for improved results in sales, and in life can come from. The sharing of best practices and the keys to success in this book are based on real world experiences and seeing the rise and fall of sales professionals, as well as human beings, as we stumble and climb our way through the game of life.

Chapter 1

Focus

Focus. Such a simple word yet filled with such great intention and energy channeled in the right direction. With the right focus and the proper motivation, a forward-thinking individual becomes unstoppable. Their resolve and commitment to follow through becomes fueled by the mission or vision they have created for themselves.

Where does this focus and drive come from? Why do some people stand out in a crowd and carry themselves with an intended focus that others just don't seem to possess?

Internally these high-achieving individuals have created their own personal mission statement. The key here is *personal*. It must be centered on your own goals and levels of achievement you want to exceed. Because the goals are personal in nature, they can take on many forms:

"I want to make $300,000 in one year by the end of my third year with my job."

"I want to purchase a home for my family and provide a life of financial stability."

"My goal is to become the number one producing sales rep in my region in one year, in my division in two years, and in the company in three years."

"I want to provide an education for my children."

"I want to create a life where I control my hours worked, and where I get back every ounce of effort I put into my job, in the form of income."

"I want to retire by fifty-five, and being a top-performing sales professional can make that happen."

"I want to buy amazing toys and live a great and prosperous life!"

The key here is to find that one thing that compels you. Find the singular point of focus that wills you to exceed even your own expected effort levels. Your personal mission statement is a powerful tool in setting the course of your own success.

Your personal mission statement is a powerful tool in setting the course of your own success.

Focus

In my years in sales leadership capacities, there is one great common denominator in those at the top, and that is they have a will to succeed that is fueled by a very personal mission statement. In some cases, they have more at stake than just themselves, and in others, it is only about themselves, but in both instances, it works because of the compelling nature of the vision they have chosen to direct their focus.

The other key variable in your focus and personal mission statement is to have vision- for the long term. It's important that your goals be realistic and attainable within a reasonable amount of time. Make your personal vision tangible, and keep it so close to your soul so you feel it, touch it, and taste it every day. In creating your vision, it is also important you keep perspective on time. How long will this take you to accomplish? Are your timelines realistic? Have you assessed all the potential pitfalls? Is the present course of action you are on and the job you have going to allow you to achieve these goals?

Make your personal vision tangible, and keep it so close to your soul so you feel it, touch it, and taste it every day.

Focus

Make sure there is realism to your timeline and to your goals. When the two come together, the ending result is a powerful motivational tool. Find that thing inside you that compels you, pushes you, and directs you. You have to set your course with the proper focus and motivation, and having the right personal mission statement and the right set of expectations around it will be the most powerful driver you can tap into.

Keep your mind engaged in the right direction. There is great value in meditation. Meditation, in my estimate, is the ability to control your mind, and keep the negative, waste minded thoughts at bay. To keep negative thoughts moving through you but not allow them to sit inside you. Create a mindful process where the negative thoughts do not take hold. It takes discipline to stay in control of the thoughts in your head, but when done well this practice will keep you focused on the variables within your control as opposed to focusing on the negativity that comes up in all of us.

control your mind

Focus

A reality to life is that those who can control their mind control the game. Controlling your mind and your focus is a powerful tool in your tool belt to create the success you desire.

Try clearing your mind and focusing only on your breath for five minutes. As thoughts come to you, recognize them, understand their genesis, and then allow them to flow through you without taking hold in your psyche.

A strong mind is essential to long-term success. Your thoughts and the words you speak into the universe carry great weight. Control your stream of consciousness, and know that through proper focus and controlling, what takes hold in your thought process and what does not, are all variables that you can control. Become a master of your thoughts and your own reactions to negative variables, and you will find yourself a more focused and resolute professional.

Of course the physical self is important but, from my experience, not nearly as important as the strengthening of your mind. Control your mind, and you will control the game. Meditate, exercise, learn, read and grow, and in time become a master of your thoughts and your focus. You have to build the skill set of clear "introspective thought." In other words, "What should I be doing differently to change my results? What is my role in my current situation, and what can I do to make it better?"

Control your mind, and you will control the game.

Focus

Being introspective and honest with yourself is a common characteristic among high-performing individuals. They have the ability to question themselves, and understand they themselves have a great deal of control of their situation day in and day out.

Stay the course you have laid out in front of you with a compelling personal mission statement, keep your mind focused in a positive direction, and be completely resolute about your desire to achieve your success. Everybody wants to win, everyone wants to find success, but so few are willing to put in the work on themselves that needs to be done in order to set the table for success.

Top performers have built a personal mission statement that is a true compelling vision, they intensify their focus by controlling the content of their own mind, and they realize the challenges they will be facing along the path to success. In this process, they have also committed to a reasonable timeline and hold themselves accountable to success measures along the timeline they have created.

Everybody wants to win, everyone wants to find success, but so few are willing to put in the work on themselves that needs to be done in order to set the table for success.

Chapter 2

The Foundation of a High Achiever

The Foundation of a High Achiever

In thirteen -plus years as a vice president of sales for three different organizations, I have been involved in the hiring of more than five-hundred-plus sales representatives, and from that segment of people, I saw people rise to great success, many mire in mediocrity, and even more fail. Finding quality talent in a professional sales environment, much to the ire of many of you reading this, becomes one of sales leadership's greatest challenges.

Finding great talent and what truly separates the exceptional from the average, in and of itself, becomes an ongoing quest for sales leadership. Great sales organizations are always willing to take on great talent. If the makeup of the individual is of the highest quality, that person will drive success regardless of challenges or circumstances they meet.

In hiring and parting ways with so many over the years, we did what we could to differentiate the exceptional from the average.

We introduced behavioral interviewing, we utilized panel interviews and interdepartmental interviews, and we utilized online competency tests, all in an effort to get feedback in order to find the top performing sales professional characteristics we were looking for.

In the quest to surround myself with the best talent we could grab, there was a trend that began to develop over the years. Initially, as much as I thought industry experience and market and competitor knowledge were of great importance, the results began to paint a different picture.

In months and years of seeing talent rise and fall, three core competencies became the foundation of the top performers that clearly rang through time and time again: drive for success, perseverance, and competitiveness above all else are the main ingredients to a high-producing sales professional.

In months and years of seeing talent rise and fall, three core competencies became the foundation of the top performers that clearly rang through time and time again: drive for success, perseverance, and competitiveness above all else are the main ingredients to a high-producing sales professional.

In one of the companies I worked for, we were able to prove this by going against industry standards and creating a college graduate program where we actively sought out recent college graduates who possessed these attributes. They had no industry experience, and they had no product knowledge, but through the interview process, we were able to ascertain if they possessed these three critical variables, and if so, we brought them into the program.

Bright young minds are able to grasp concepts and value propositions, and especially technology, very readily. We engrossed the young sales talent into the culture of the company and a full product-training regimen for one continuous month. We armed them with the ability to overcome the common objections they would face, and make them experts on our product within the months' time. After one year of employment, the turnover and the performance was at par and, in some cases, above what industry veterans had produced in the same time frame.

It's not the industry experience, or even

It's not the industry experience, or even the rolodex, that forms the foundation of high achievers but the core intangible competencies of drive, perseverance, and competitiveness.

the rolodex, that forms the foundation of high achievers but the core intangible competencies of drive, perseverance, and competitiveness. With those characteristics firmly implanted into your psyche, you can become a masterful salesperson and earn a living far above your peers in different professions and build a quality of life that affords you the flexibility and autonomy you desire.

With that knowledge in tow, it's important to completely understand what each of these competencies looks like.

People who are loaded with drive push themselves continually. They meet adversity and challenge head on. People with this trait are always questioning themselves in the process. They are very introspective people because they are constantly questioning their role in their results. They have a done a deep dive into the fundamentals of their role, the blocking and tackling of success. It may look like setting appointments, making more calls, getting themselves in front of the decision maker, and putting forth a level of effort that is likely unmatched through 90 percent of their sales organization.

Their phone is always on, their mind is always at work, and their focus lies steadfastly ahead. The day-to-day grind of the job does not affect them in the same way it does the midlevel and low-level performers. Part of their drive is the vision for the long term. They understand the work that needs to be put in day after day after day. Sales is a wonderful profession because of the autonomy it can provide, but that same autonomy is the ultimate failure of so many in the business because they lack the discipline to manage themselves. Keeping a solid daily structure, a true recipe for success, is at the core of driven individuals. Those who lack this same drive leave the house late, arrive home early, and find moments to mentally "check out" while they curse their results at month end and look to place blame on the market, the competition, or lack of training.

Sales is a wonderful profession because of the autonomy it can provide, but that same autonomy is the ultimate failure of so many in the business because they lack the discipline to manage themselves.

Driven people find the threshold where others fold, and push through it. They also understand the numbers behind the success. They realize how many calls it will take, how many appointments need to be set, and how thoroughly they need to follow up to create their success. They are a student of their product and the industry, look for ways to educate themselves beyond the obvious, and place themselves in a position of value by the knowledge they carry and the service levels they provide. Nothing can stop a driven individual armed with a moderately competitive product and the support necessary to create the success they long to attain.

Driven people find the threshold
where others fold, and push through it.

The second pillar of strength for high achievers is perseverance. I recall a conversation with one of our top-performing reps and asking them questions about their success. In my career, I have always sought out top performers because they have so much value to share. Oftentimes my role in sales leadership was to simply gain an understanding of what worked best in the marketplace from our top performers, ensure I could also execute and drive success in the same manner, and then share this information throughout the organization. This was the basis for the synergy we were able to create throughout our sales culture. It was during one of these conversations when I learned something very valuable in the makeup for top performers.

When I asked him why he thought people failed, his reply was, "They can't take the no's."

I thought about that for a moment, and then he went on. "So many people come here thinking that it is easy, and they are going to make big money in a faster amount of time than anyone else ever has. They get met with objections and challenges and the no's, and then they fade away as quickly as they came."

This became an important revelation in the quest to understand high achievers. Perseverance. Perseverance is the ability to pursue everything with energy and the need to see things through to the finish, even through the most difficult of situations. People filled with this trait rarely give up, especially in the face of challenge and setbacks. To this select group of people, the setbacks become stepping stones. To those outside of this group looking in, the challenges and setbacks become insurmountable obstacles that ultimately lead to their demise.

These individuals blame the product, the competition, or the market. This typically occurs because the ego of most sales professionals does not allow them to look inward at themselves and their role in their results. How you meet obstacles, how you overcome objections, how you carry yourself in the face of adversity are all variables you can control, and all exist at very high levels for high-earning sales professionals.

How you meet obstacles, how you overcome objections, how you carry yourself in the face of adversity are all variables you can control, and all exist at very high levels for high-earning sales professionals.

People who are long in perseverance fuel their vision for the long term and the understanding of their role in their results. They realize that service levels are of great importance, and they understand the numbers behind the success. They focus on the variables within their control and remain focused on the "blocking and tackling" of calls to current and new customers, and the impact of effective appointments with the right decision makers. They carry integrity and a self-driven strength of character with them at all times. They live by their own set of core values they have instilled in themselves. Top performers have an incredible sense of self, and the understanding of how properly executing day in and day out will lead to the levels of success they desire to achieve.

If you ever have the opportunity, read the book *Good to Great*. There was a time it was on every executive's desk in the late 90s and early 2000s. The book outlines the differentiating factors from companies that were on a level of "good" success and then in time outdistanced their competitive segment to produce "great" results. One of the concepts that have always stuck with me from the book is the "Stockdale paradox."

Top performers have an incredible sense of self, and the understanding of how properly executing day in and day out will lead to the levels of success they desire to achieve.

This paradox is named for Admiral Stockdale, who was a prisoner of war as an officer for eight years during the Vietnam War. He was tortured more than twenty times and was never given much reason for him to ever believe that he would live through the ordeal to see his wife and family again. But during his captivity, Admiral Stockdale never doubted that he would get out and prevail in the end. Not only prevail, but know that in the end this would be the defining moment of his life that would forever change him for the better.

Then comes the paradox: while Stockdale had remarkable faith in his ability to persevere, he discovered it was always the most optimistic of his fellow prisoners who failed to make it out alive.

"They were the ones who said, 'We're going to be out by Christmas.' And Christmas would come, and Christmas would go. Then they'd say, 'We're going to be out by Easter.' And Easter would come, and Easter would go. And then Thanksgiving, and then it would be Christmas again. And they died of a broken spirit."

What Admiral Stockdale displayed was unwavering perseverance in his own knowledge that in the end he was going to make it and be a better person for it, but there would be great challenge along the way. He realized that during his ordeal, every day was going to be a fight for his life. He met every day with a great resolve and understanding of the challenges he would meet that particular day. In doing so day by day, challenge after challenge, and adversity after adversity, he met them all. And through his knowledge of the day-to-day challenges he faced, underneath he maintained his undying belief in his ability to succeed in the end.

The Foundation of a High Achiever

The third pedestal in the foundation of high achievers is competitiveness. For people in the sales profession this is a bit of a given, but a true competitive spirit is omnipresent in high achievers. Not only in just the obvious of being the number 1 sales rep in a region, a division, or the country but in being competitive with yourself. High achievers are well versed in introspective thought. "What could I have done differently in that meeting? What I could have said differently, how I could have overcame that objection better, what I not know about the competition, what new things are happening in the industry that I need to learn."

High achievers are well versed in introspective thought.

To be truly competitive is to win the battle of your own mind. Control your mind, control your actions, and compete with your inner-self every day, and you will build success.

Competitors not only compete with their peers for rankings but also, with themselves to improve each and every day. I have yet to meet an omnipotent individual in any of my dealings. I have met people who do believe they have most if not all the answers, and those are not people I feel a desire to build a relationship with. Top performers compete with their inner voice; they learn daily to better themselves, to improve on their execution and learn from the top performers around them. To be truly competitive is to win the battle of your own mind. Control your mind, control your actions, and compete with your inner-self every day, and you will build success.

Chapter 3

Knowing What Success Looks Like

Knowing what success looks like is singular to the sales profession or corporation that you are affiliated with; however, the core of success reaches across the needs of all industries in any sales organization. So how do you find what success looks like in your particular scenario? Look no further than the top of your rankings on your own production reports or revenue reports or closed sales reports that your company uses to measure success.

Knowing What Success Looks Like

It sounds simple, but so few sales professionals take the time to reach out to the top performers at their own company. High performers are willing to talk and share, but they will not reach out to you first. Seek them out, and learn the valuable insight that they carry with them. Find out the fundamentals of how they created their success:

- How long did it take to create their success?
- What are the three most important things they like to accomplish each day?
- How do they structure their week?
- How do they structure their month?
- What are the details of how they do what they do?
- How do they overcome common objections?
- How do they sell against the competition?
- How did they build their large accounts?

  How do they sustain their results?

High performers are willing to talk and share, but they will not reach out to you first.

Ask questions of them. Offer to ride with them or sit side by side, and shadow them for a day, or even two days, if you can. Most organizational change comes from someone doing something slightly different that gets a somewhat better result. There are not monumental changes that lead to dramatic variances in your results. Their skill sets and daily habits are built over time and oftentimes are just slight variations of what already is being done. You need to learn their nuances, their differences, how and where and why they execute day in and day out in the manner that they do.

One of the key variables here is the fundamental behaviors of their role that they have developed. How many calls in a day, how many customers they contact, who they contact, the content of what they say, the manner in which they carry themselves the people they make sure to speak with on a regular basis all are difference makers in their results. The blocking and tackling (fundamentals) should be your primary focus. Sales and sales results are a numbers business, and top performers understand that.

Most organizational change comes from someone doing something slightly different that gets a somewhat better result.

If 20 percent of your contacts turn into accounts and 30 percent of those accounts turn into valuable producers, then work the math backward. So if you are going to capture two out of ten contacts and get three out of ten of those to turn into high-producing accounts, then input the numbers you need in each instance to exceed the current pace or run rate of production.

This is often where high performers begin to separate themselves. They will contact twenty to thirty potential new prospects in a day, where the average producer will contact fifteen to twenty. Typically, high performers carry higher penetration numbers on the accounts they do establish. Learn why that is, and ask questions how they do it.

If they penetrate 37 percent of the accounts they establish while the rest of the sales force is at 30 percent, know the nuances of how they got there and then emulate that. The high producers in your region, your state, your division, or your company carry higher closing ratios. Top performers have done the work they needed to do initially by outworking the rest of the sales force in the form of contacts and accounts earned, and then watched their closing ratios separate from the rest of the group by the service levels and value they provide.

Top performers have done the work they needed to do initially by outworking the rest of the sales force in the form of contacts and accounts earned, and then watched their closing ratios separate from the rest of the group by the service levels and value they provide.

Knowing What Success Looks Like

Even more importantly, high performers live the value of superior service. In time, they have become industry and competition experts through their desire to learn more about their markets and the space they are in. The follow-up from high performers outshines the follow-up of middle of the pack performers. Their phone is always on, and their word to their customers carries weight. They take on the difficult questions and challenges head on, and if they don't know the answer at the time, they take the steps to learn the answers and then quickly get back to their account.

Never underestimate the value of superior service while carrying great integrity and strength of character. People are drawn to those attributes, and continuing to carry yourself in that manner will win the minds and hearts of customers in the end. Yes, your product needs to be in a certain bandwidth of competitiveness; however, the controllable variables such as knowledge, service, integrity, effort, and follow through will win the respect and the business of your newfound clients.

Never underestimate the value of superior service while carrying great integrity and strength of character. People are drawn to those attributes, and continuing to carry yourself in that manner will win the minds and hearts of customers in the end.

High performers also carry with them the knowledge that building success is a process. There needs to be work done every day, and the foundation is built brick by brick, call by call, pitch by pitch. Success builds with singles and doubles, not hitting home runs on every account. This can occur during the process of building and selling accounts, but the top performers know not to count on it, and when they do build that big account, they continue to search for other opportunities because they understand the risks that lie with so much of their production coming from one account. They are always focused on the future and what the next month will bring based upon their actions and efforts during the month prior.

Success is the sum of great efforts executed day in and day out, and once you've walked that path daily for a period of time, your foundation for success begins to build, and in time with a series of progressions that are executed day in and day out, your production and your results and your income will grow along with it.

The reality is that everyone wants to win, everyone wants to be at the top, but few are truly willing to put forth the time and effort and work that it takes to get there. It is the day-to-day blocking and tackling, the understanding of the numbers of the variables that drive results, and instituting a plan around them. Your success is built in the day-to-day actions or inactions that you take, the moment-to-moment decisions that you make. Results are not built on hope, or worry, or handouts, or complaining about your current situation; your results are built squarely upon your efforts. Take the time to fully understand the areas you need to be applying your efforts.

Your success is built in the day-to-day actions or inactions that you take, the moment-to-moment decisions that you make. Results are not built on hope, or worry, or handouts, or complaining about your current situation; your results are built squarely upon your efforts.

Chapter 4

Know Yourself

Know Yourself

The challenge with sales professionals is that large egos often come in tow alongside talent and a track record of success. Although certain levels of ego can be a positive variable in your results in the form of quiet confidence and steadfast belief in one's abilities to prevail, ego can also be the ultimate blinder to forward progress.

Egos cause issues when they allow people to fall into the "victim" mind-set, meaning their current state of production is predicated on things outside of their control: "The market is slow, the competition is too stiff, I started this job at the wrong time, and the other reps have all the good accounts." The challenge of looking inward is constant, and those who do it well, who truly understand how they are and who they are, are the people who create their own successes.

It's important to have great self-awareness when you feel yourself slipping down the wrong path. There are a lot of negative salespeople and, for that matter, just straight-out negative people in the world. The reality is we truly don't see things as they are; we see things as *we* are. Meaning our perceptions drive our realities, and if your perception is that you've been dealt a bad hand and there are too many variables outside of your control that are hindering your success, then that is exactly the current state of affairs that you exist in.

Be aware of the people whom you surround yourself with and the type of feedback or energy drain they bring to your day. Stay steadfastly focused on the variables within your control: who you call, how you call, what you say, and becoming an even greater student of your industry and the values of the product you are selling.

Be aware of the people whom you surround yourself with and the type of feedback or energy drain they bring to your day. Stay steadfastly focused on the variables within your control

---

Know Yourself

When you feel your personal reserves starting to slip, take a look at the long term. Assess what you are doing each and every day, and know that if you continue on a path of good fundamentals each and every day, your results will turn in the direction you want them to go. The reality is that success takes work, and those at the top have found a way to squeeze more out of their day and stay focused on the long-term objectives. Their service levels are at the top of the industry, and the value they have created for themselves begins to precede them in the industry. Customers see it in their eyes and the confidence with which they carry themselves, and both the top sales rep and customer alike know this person can be counted on for all aspects of the sale from start to finish, and beyond.

The difference you make in the world is determined by the moment-to-moment decisions that you make, the actions or the inactions that you take. That is what begins to separate high performers from the rest. Know when your reserves are low, and know when you are not channeling your efforts in the right direction.

The difference you make in the world is determined by the moment-to-moment decisions that you make, the actions or the inactions that you take.

Know Yourself

Check your ego at the door, and ask questions. Ask questions of the top performers around you, and work together with your sales manager to hammer out a strategy you will execute above and beyond each and every day.

Know you are the key variable in your results, know when it is time to ask for help, and know when it is time to attack your day, your week, and your month differently. Top performers have an acute sense of self in regards to their role in their results and what they need to be doing each and every hard-fought day in order to create the level of production they desire.

Chapter 5

Overcome Adversity

Overcome Adversity

I've read commentary in the past that suggests that on average we face twenty-three adversarial situations in any given day. Someone cuts you off in traffic, you spill your coffee on your lap, your spouse is upset at you as you leave the house in the morning, you set the wrong time on your calendar for an important meeting, and on and on life's little and large adversities go.

This certainly isn't a new concept, but the thought process does carry a significant amount of weight: what separates the exceptional from the average is how they respond to adversity. Life and sales is not about what happens to you, it's about how you overcome the challenges and obstacles you face each and every day. The greater the adversity, the more focus and resolve you need to keep your mind-set in the right place and stay focused on the variables you can control, and channel your energies in that direction.

Life and sales is not about what happens to you, it's about how you overcome the challenges and obstacles you face each and every day.

Overcome Adversity

The impact of adversity is individual. Adversity is as individual as our own perceptions in life. Meaning one person's challenge may seem insignificant to some but be received as a tremendous hurdle to others. It is those times, when our own perceptions create such monumental challenges, that we need to understand our roles in how we process the current challenge or adversity that we are facing.

I am not one to judge people's own developed levels of adversity they have assigned to various obstacles in life, but as a sales leader, I have seen the toll on results of good salespeople because the current adversity they are in begins to swallow them whole. There is one thing I can guarantee you in life, and that is you will face adversity: divorce, loss of job, loss of love, loss of a loved one, illness, major accidents, etcetera, etcetera.

There is one thing I can guarantee you in life, and that is you will face adversity

---

These are all significant adversities that will sideline the best of producers; however, I'm not necessarily speaking to these life-changing moments, I am speaking more toward the challenges you face day to day. In these instances, I find mid-tier and bottom-tier performing sales reps spin completely out of control over a lost account, a botched meeting, the competition, the perceived value of the product they represent, and the list goes on.

This is where you begin to see the separation of the high producers from the rest of the pack. It is these challenges that hammer away at the wills of the less focused but serve as a stepping stone for those who meet these types of challenges head on, quickly address the situation, correct it, or just move on to the next opportunity.

In hiring sales reps, over time, I noticed a pattern began to develop. Whenever I would interview candidates who have this very high energy and over-the-top positive personality, I would find that these types of individuals would fade during times of adversity. I call it the "cheerleader effect," and it impacts both males and females. They present themselves with great energy and positivity, and by the end of the interview, they are exhaling deeply, and I can almost imagine the sigh of relief once they have finished the interview.

I had one candidate whom I had interviewed and later parted ways with who told me my interview with her was exhausting and she gave it everything she had to ensure it went well. What I've discovered with these personality types is that what goes up eventually comes down. Meaning they don't operate within a tighter functioning emotional bandwidth. With the extreme highs come the extreme lows. Their attitude and energy is up, and then with what they perceive as a few too many adversities or obstacles to success, they quickly dive down to thoughts of despair and then begin looking for reasons why their results or current situation has fallen off.

The other challenge with these personality types is they are quick to enter the "victim" mindset, put on their Teflon armor, and begin to place blame elsewhere rather than look to themselves for what they could be doing differently to improve their situation.

High-performing sales professionals operate within a much-narrower bandwidth of energy and emotion. They are not derailed by the lesser adversities in life and always keep moving forward and questioning how they can do things differently. There is a certain quiet confidence that comes from life experiences and understanding how life and the world work. In life, you have to understand that adversity is inevitable, and you have to find a way to manage yourself and your bandwidth of emotions as you work through the adversities you will face in life and in your profession.

High-performing sales professionals operate within a much-narrower bandwidth of energy and emotion. They are not derailed by the lesser adversities in life and always keep moving forward and questioning how they can do things differently.

Overcome Adversity

I like to reflect on Jackie Robinson when I think of how people can positively respond to adversity. I have a feeling that Jackie didn't wake up each day thinking life was going to be a bed of roses as he stepped onto the field. The racism, the bigotry, the hatred he faced was enormous, and likely would have crushed the vast majority of people who would have faced those same adversities. Yet Jackie Robinson overcame. Not only did he overcome his adversities but also he went on to become one of the greatest to ever play the game.

Try to place some perspective around the adversity you face in life. How bad is it really? How can you manage yourself differently when you meet adversity, and which adversities carry weight and which do not? You have to be able to deal with the "challenges of life." There is one thing that life will teach you, and that is that you have to manage yourself well through the "worst of it," because its involvement in your life is not a potential occurrence, it is the reality of life itself.

How well you manage yourself through

your daily, weekly, and monthly challenges affects yourself in so many ways. Realize what the adversity is and its origins as you meet it, and learn in time to manage yourself with a narrower bandwidth of emotion and focused resolve, as you press through the challenges you face each and every day. High-performing sales professionals, and those who seem to always excel at life, are people who have mastered the art and learned skill of overcoming adversity.

Chapter 6

Empower Yourself

T o empower yourself in the sales profession means you give yourself the right, or the power, to take full control of your actions, which drive your results. The path to success in sales is lined with data:

- How many calls does it take to generate an appointment?

- How many appointments does it take to land an account?

- How many meetings does it take to convert your account into a strong producer?

- How many opportunities exist in a designated area?

- What percent of those opportunities have been contacted?

- What percent of those that have been contacted are still not converted to accounts?

- How many accounts do you need to generate the level of success you are looking for?

- How many self-driven activities is it going to take each day to create the results you want?

You need to understand the data behind the success. Each sales organization will typically use some variation of a CRM, and what so many sales professionals fail to realize is that the data behind the results clearly lights the path for the success you desire. Take the time to analyze the top performers in your region and understand the measurements behind their success. What are their closing ratios, how many calls do they make in a day, week, or month? How many accounts do they have, and how long did it take to build those accounts? Which people do they generally contact first, which people do they work with as they account builds into a high producer?

Become a student of the metrics behind the results, and then model your behaviors after those metrics. Once you understand the basic

Become a student of the metrics behind the results, and then model your behaviors after those metrics. Once you understand the basic fundamental math of how top producers execute, you become empowered.

fundamental math of how top producers execute, you become empowered. You become empowered because you now know exactly how many calls, how many appointments, and how many accounts you need to drive your success. Now you begin to wrestle control back into your favor because the results behind the data show you what needs to be done. Now the ball is in your court; now you need to execute.

You would think that armed with the data of what top performers look like that it would be much easier from that point forward. But the reality is we as individuals still need to execute day in and day out, and that is where the separation of high performers to midrange producers begins. It begins with the "self." The reality is that the path to generate the metrics behind the results often requires a great deal of effort and determination to work through the challenging times. In that process, sales professionals will still fall to the "victim" mind-set as they look for reasons why their metrics are not meeting up with those of the top performers.

Empower Yourself

An even more critical variable to the separation between the exceptional and the average is belief. Belief in the competitiveness of the product, belief in the results behind the metrics, belief in the viability of the market, these are all critical variables to your success. Without belief in these areas, your results will slide, your confidence will wane, and now you can point your finger elsewhere for blame regarding your results.

Do not underestimate the power of belief and what belief can do to create your success. Consider the story of Roger Bannister. Roger Bannister was the first human being on the planet to run a mile in less than four minutes. Roger accomplished this feat on May 6, 1954, and prior to that day, people had been trying to break the four-minute mile for decades. It had come to the point where medical doctors determined the human physiology would not allow the mechanics of the body to achieve such an accomplishment. Sportswriters, fellow athletes, and people around the world built up a belief that running a mile in less than four minutes simply was not possible.

Do not underestimate the power of belief and what belief can do to create your success.

Empower Yourself

Roger Bannister held a different belief system, and pushed himself and his work and preparation to break the new record, harder than he ever had in his life. Roger put forth the work needed to accomplish his goal, and then on that fateful day, he crossed the finish line at three minutes, 59.4 seconds, and belief mechanisms were forever changed. Once Mr. Bannister proved it could be done, his record lasted a brief forty-six days until his time was bested. Multiple runners over the course of the next year continued to fall below the four-minute mark, and now the record stands at three minutes 43.13 seconds. Because of the belief people possess in themselves and the process of preparation, and their ability to put forth the work necessary to be champion, this record will undoubtedly be broken again.

Empower yourself with data and the metrics behind the success. Then empower your mind with belief in the value of what it is you are selling and the potential for success within the market you serve. Once you have grasped these concepts, nothing can get in the way of your results.

Chapter 7

Know Your Value Add

Know Your Value Add

U nderstanding the value you bring to the table is yet another key variable in the recipe for success for high-performing sales professionals. In other words, why do you matter? Why are you different than the myriad of other sales reps who have come before you? How do you differentiate yourself from the rest of the pack? Top producers have a way of distancing themselves in several areas:

- Understanding how their service and follow-up creates value

- The ability to comfortably build personally connected relationships

- Product knowledge

- Competitor knowledge

- Industry knowledge

When you first approach a potential new account, it is important that you ask specific questions and listen more than you speak. On several occasions, I have witnessed sales reps open the meeting by selling and quickly getting into their perceived value proposition and then droning on about features and benefits before even asking one single question. The key is to ask enough questions to understand the area of need your potential client may have. Learn what open-ended questions create the best dialogue, and use their responses to build your value proposition. The more your client speaks, the more sales opportunities they begin to present to you. Once you have opened a good dialogue, you then begin to build the conversation around the needs they have expressed, through the questions you have asked:

- Tell me a little about the current provider, where do you see the greatest value they provide?

- How long have you been with them, and what keeps you connected?

- Are there any segments of business you would like to see improved?

- What, if any, pain points have you experienced in dealing with any providers?

- What aspects of your business would you like to improve on?

- Are you reaching or exceeding your current goals?

- What aspects of what you do derail you from focusing on revenue-generating activity?

The list of questions goes on and on. Consult with your sales leaders, and once again learn from the high performers in your region about what questions they ask of new clients. Build a great question list, and continue to place yourself into uncomfortable situations until you master the skill of asking great questions. When you ask great fact-finding questions, the solutions to gaining your clients business begin to present themselves, and now you begin to truly understand the "value add" you can bring to your client.

Let's expand on "uncomfortable situations."

Know Your Value Add

Placing yourself in front of difficult clients or hard sells is where your growth begins to build. The more uncomfortable situations you face, the more belief you begin to build in yourself and the product or company you are representing. It is always easy to close the lay-down customer, or to service a long-standing relationship you have built, but the real growth, the real improvement, the true building of your personal value add comes from you growing through the difficult challenges. Your professional growth comes from your learning, and your learning compounds as you become more and more comfortable regardless of the situation that you face.

When you ask great fact-finding questions, the solutions to gaining your clients business begin to present themselves, and now you begin to truly understand the "value add" you can bring to your client.

Know Your Value Add

How you prepare for conversations is another learned skill of top producers. Great conversation is an art. It's a developed skill. How many times do you play out conversations with a client before they occur? It's having a game plan. Just as any football or basketball coach prepares for an opponent, you too should prepare for your meetings and phone calls. Anticipate what you expect them to say, and be prepared in advance for how you will respond so it appears effortless to your potential client.

Even more important, it is critical that you understand all potential objections you may face. Once you understand all of the objections, and have talked through, written out, or role-played through the objections, only then will you be truly focused on the value you can provide. Who you speak to, how you communicate, how you prepare for each and every conversation are tremendous ways in which you begin to build value and create high performing results. Become a true sales professional by understanding at least three critical components of what it is that you represent that adds value to your customers, and become a master of those variables:

Great conversation is an art.

Know Your Value Add

- Know your product.

- Know your competition.

- Know your industry.

- Know the objections you will face.

- Carry great belief in yourself and what you represent.

- Prepare for each and every conversation you have with your client base.

When you can do these things well, you now have built value in not only the company or product you represent but also in you as an integral part of the success of your client. In time, the value you provide as an individual becomes primary to the product you represent. Build yourself into the culture of the client you are building the relationship with, by the value that you provide as an individual. When you do this well, you will build a customer for life, and your results grow exponentially.

Build yourself into the culture of the client you are building the relationship with, by the value that you provide as an individual.

Chapter 8

Create Your Change

Create Your Change

I don't believe that anyone has ever stated it better or more succinctly than Gandhi himself: "Become the change you want to see." So simplistic, so altruistic, yet so difficult for so many to master. Truly embracing that level of change, almost down to the cellular level, takes a great deal of introspective thought. It takes a great deal of understanding of what we have done as individuals to create our current set of circumstances. In order to truly change the course of ourselves, and the course of our results, we need to truly embrace the change needed within ourselves.

The reality is that as we walk through the world, we really don't see things as they are, we see things as we are. Meaning the projection of our own thoughts and beliefs and perceptions tend to cloud every encounter we create.

Create Your Change

The reality is that as we walk through the world, we really don't see things as they are, we see things as we are. Meaning the projection of our own thoughts and beliefs and perceptions tend to cloud every encounter we create. To truly be still and listen with an open mind and an open heart takes a great deal of focus and thought. Once we truly open ourselves up to the fact that we do not have all the answers and that the only steadfast way to create change in our results is to work on the changes needed inside of us, enlightenment will soon follow. In doing so, we grow and evolve as people because now we become students of life and teachers of our own selves. Real growth and real development has to come from a place of internal acceptance. Without truly believing deep within ourselves about the changes that we as individuals need to embark upon to create change, we will never truly realize our full potential. We must become the change we want to see.

So what will you do differently to create the change within yourself to drive the change in your results and in your life? Herein lies the challenge. For now we begin to realize that to create change in our results we need to build a platform within us that allows us to accept the fact that we need to change in order to change the direction of our results and our lives.

One simple change could be that moving forward you will make five extra phone calls per day, and work to create at least one additional appointment per day. Think about the impact to your results by you making the effort to create the additional opportunities to be successful. If you have done the work to learn the value your product has to offer and then focus on the differentiating factors that you bring to the table to create your own personal value, then simply by executing at a higher level via your own actions, you will undoubtedly create the change in your results and in your life that you are seeking.

Most organizational change comes from someone doing something slightly different that creates a somewhat better result. Now once those slight changes are shared and executed on a wider scale, then change in results begins to occur on a macro scale. All simply because someone took

---

Most organizational change comes from someone doing something slightly different that creates a somewhat better result.

---

the initiative to approach the current situation a bit differently and realize the positive change their own actions created.

So what is the one thing you can do differently to drive change within you and your results? Here begins your new challenge; for a new behavior to become a habit, it needs to be repeated twenty-seven times. Think about that for a moment. Think about how many times you have embarked on the journey of change only to be met with challenge early on in the process that allowed you to accept your old ways of thinking or executing as once again the status quo.

Challenge and obstacles come in sales just as they do in life. Here is yet another opportunity to persevere through the obstacles that life presents, knowing that by embarking upon this change ultimately your long-term results will benefit. But you have to work through the challenges and have enough foresight to understand that change does not come easy, but ultimately change is what builds upon the greatness you are looking to achieve. It requires fortitude to continue your change journey. It requires effort and long-term vision for the future and belief in yourself and what it is that you represent.

Everyone thinks of changing the
world, but so few think of changing
themselves.

Create Your Change

Everyone thinks of changing the world, but so few think of changing themselves. When you think about it, it's easy to want to change big issues in the world and in life. Politics, world peace, your favorite teams coach, et cetera, et cetera. Those types of changes are easy because we truly have little to no impact on the outcome of those types of desired changes, but we certainly can wish or hope for those types of changes.

The challenging changes we need to make are the changes within ourselves. That requires even greater work because it takes a willingness to truly understand we should be doing things differently, and that we truly are the reason we have come to this point in our lives. That is the hard work, that is the scary work, and that is the work that truly needs to be done. When you work on positive change within yourself, your perspective on how we walk through the world begins to change itself. Our relationships become stronger, we have less stress in our lives, and we have greater clarity on what needs to be done. All this comes about through the internal changes we make.

Create Your Change

You first have to be big enough to realize you need to make a change within yourself. Then you have to work through the obstacles and passivity that will come up within yourself to truly create the change within you that is needed to build the success in your career and within your life. Become the change you wish to see.

Chapter 9

Walk the Talk

At this stage in the game of sales and success, you've likely armed yourself with a great deal of information about how to execute, and done some work on understanding the process and daily expectations necessary to create the success you are looking for. If you are reading this, you've likely already embarked on your sales career, or you've been working in this profession for several years and are now looking for that edge to move the needle on your results to the next level. It could be that even prior to reading this you already fully understood the blocking and tackling of your world needed to drive every bit of success you generate out of your market.

So what has left you mired in your current level of productivity? It's the internal call to action that compels you to fully execute your plan. It's taking that first step, it's putting one foot in front of the other and continuing to do so day in and day out. It's doing the work necessary to drive your success.

It's time to "walk the talk." At this stage in the game, it truly can become the most difficult leg in your journey toward success, or it becomes the most empowering step you've yet to take. Now you have armed yourself with knowledge: knowledge of the process, knowledge of how the top performers in your world achieved their success, knowledge of what you now must do today, tomorrow, next week, next month, and on and on it goes.

Now you yourself need to become more than just another person who gave up that easily. Now you need to instill your new beliefs and understanding and make them your daily success habits. You have to push yourself to improve every day, put yourself into uncomfortable moments so you learn and grow and improve based on those new experiences.

You need to understand what success truly looks like and compile the knowledge you have gained and put forth the effort to create your success. You need to become a better you.

You need to understand what success truly looks like and compile the knowledge you have gained and put forth the effort to create your success. You need to become a better you. You yourself need to be accountable for your actions and execution. You must hold yourself to a higher standard of performance than anyone has set for you. It is time for you to walk the talk of success and improve yourself and your results by your actions each and every day.

I often reflect back to an annual sales conference where an individual left an indelible impression upon me that to this day I have not forgotten. In my roles as vice president of sales, I took very active roles in setting agendas and facilitating and speaking at annual sales conferences. Sales conferences are a time for sales rep to get excited about the direction the company is going, and participate in a forum where best practices can be shared and all attendees can hear directly from the top executives about the future of the organization and the role and expectations of the sales force in the company's future.

This particular conference occurred at a time when the economy was just beginning to take a downturn. We were not fully in the down cycle, but you could just begin to feel the potential impact that was on the horizon. The market was changing, and in some areas, results were flattening, while in others we were able to maintain mild to moderate growth.

In the late afternoon of the first day, I was approached by a sales representative who had been with the organization for a long time. (In some cases, longtime sales professionals with the same entity can become a bit of a challenge. In time they have created their own process in which they have driven a level of success that appeals to them, and because of the comfort zone they have created, they feel like they are operating on all cylinders and doing everything within their power to drive their results. These individuals tend not to see any changes needed within them before it is too late, and they view themselves as victims of variables outside of their control.)

This particular individual was quite

passionate upon his approach, and quickly started a conversation with me about his market, the competition, and his results.

"Kyle, I don't understand. I've been doing business the way I've been doing business for the past seven years, yet my results have gone down. I have not changed a single thing in the way that I operate, I continue to do what I have always done, and now look where my results are. What is the company going to do about it?"

I thought about his question for a moment and took a deep internal breath. "So just so I understand, you have been operating the same way for the last seven years, and you have not changed yet your results have fallen. Is that correct?"

"Yes."

"So the market, has changed, the competition has changed, the entire environment around you has changed, and you have done nothing to change how you execute, and you have watched your results slide and now you are waiting for the cavalry to come charging down the hill to change your results?"

He thought about his reply for a moment and then stated, "I guess maybe I should take a look at how I am approaching my market."

I smiled and agreed and gave him some words of encouragement and watched as he turned and walked away to reflect upon our conversation, knowing all too well it was unlikely he would ever make the internal changes necessary to create the change in his results.

Herein lies the precipice for change and the catalyst for creating your own success. As your market changes, as the competition changes, as the world around you changes, you too need to change. It's important that you be flexible enough to have an awareness of your environment and make the necessary adjustments to continue to drive results as the market around you adjusts to the current environment. You may need to find new accounts, to explore other avenues of the products you represent to find niches the market will bear. You need to execute on a different level than you were before and continue to "walk the talk" of success.

As your market changes, as the competition changes, as the world around you changes, you too need to change. It's important that you be flexible enough to have an awareness of your environment and make the necessary adjustments to continue to drive results as the market around you adjusts to the current environment.

Now is the time to look for at least three things you can be doing differently to create change in your results. The important thing here is not to give up so easily. Remember that for change to take hold, you need to repeat the new behavior time and time again until it becomes habit. Realize that through the process of finding new avenues to create new success, not every effort will be successful initially, but that does not mean it is not the right thing to do. You have to drive through the personal barriers you have created in the past to create new habits to drive your new and improved success.

Find your reason, find that inner voice, find that internal spark, and change your perspective and outlook on your career and in your life. Your perspective is a living and breathing entity, and you must cultivate and grow your focus and vision and outlook on life and success. Create the change within yourself to create the change in your results.

Find your reason, find that inner voice, find that internal spark, and change your perspective and outlook on your career and in your life. Your perspective is a living and breathing entity, and you must cultivate and grow your focus and vision and outlook on life and success. Create the change within yourself to create the change in your results.

Walk the Talk

Walk the talk of success, with every breath and with every step, and know that the journey may be hard at times but you ultimately control your own success by your own thoughts and actions in life. Your words and your thoughts carry a great deal of weight in the world that you create around you. Be aware of your thoughts and the words that you speak. Create the new direction you are seeking, through awareness of the words you say and the thoughts inside of your head. Bend your future to your will. Controlling your thoughts and carefully selecting your words, staying moment focused, and new success patterns will merge and will greatly assist you in bending your future to your will. Speak and think the success you wish to create, and in doing so, you will help manifest the future you desire.

Chapter 10

Balance

Balance

As innocuous as the concept of balance may seem when it comes to driving improved results and creating success in your career and in life, in all reality, it is likely one of the most important variables. Oftentimes driven, hard-charging individuals struggle to find balance within their life. You have to be careful not to be consumed with only one dimension of your life. The quest for balance requires active thought and participation and a willingness to carve out the balance necessary for long-term sustained success.

My belief is that the great balancing act of life consists of career, health, and family. The career dimension is obvious; however, I also believe what may look like a successful healthy career to one person may not be the same for another individual. If you choose to be a construction worker, or a teacher, or a gardener and you have a passion and appreciation for it and love what you do, then you are light-years ahead of most.

My belief is that the great balancing act of life consists of career, health, and family.

Balance

Embrace your career path, and work on becoming the best in that role that you can be. Love what you do and laugh often. Never underestimate the value of a good laugh and the healing qualities it can bring you. Enjoy your peers and your work, and build camaraderie through passion for the job and enjoyment within yourself.

Having a healthy, supporting, loving family in your world is the backbone to continuity in your life. A loving and caring partner who actively listens and supports your dreams and goals is the added variable that carries you through the adversities of your day, your week, and your month. Be sure to find time to invest in your children, if you have them. Work to be actively engaged in their schoolwork, or be active in youth sports or clubs they enjoy being a part of. The time of your children's youth will be over in the blink of an eye, and each day that you can connect with them in any sort of way is a cherished moment that fuels your passion and joy of life.

It may be that you enjoy being single or your kids are grown or have no desire for kids. In that case, cultivate deep relationships with friends and create a home environment that you love to come home to. Travel, toys, concerts, events, friends, church, the temple. Invest the time in that family of fellowship you have created, and draw upon the positive feelings inside you that the family that you have created generates. Find a harmonious balance with your family however you define it.

Your health is your future; it is your life. Without good health, all the work you have done in career and family is all for nothing if your life is untimely taken from you due to an unhealthy lifestyle. Take your spirits in moderation, and take the time to laugh and have fun, but be conscious of the need to temper your "play."

Find the time to exercise; you need to build a structure into your life that allows you to care for your body. Exercise can strengthen your body, clear your mind, and help move stress and anxiety from your body. You will look better and feel better. Your family and your career all depend on your good health, so take time to invest in yourself and work to strengthen your mind and body.

Balance

Meditation is the ability to clear your mind and control the thoughts that flow through your consciousness. Find a quick and easy book on meditation, and learn the art of clearing your mind and controlling your thoughts.

A good diet, structured exercise, and active meditation will add years to your life and bring focus and clarity to your actions in your career.

Recently, I attended an event in which Eckhart Tolle spoke. Eckhart, being the sublime thinker he is, was asked, "Of all the accomplishments in your life, what are you most proud of?"

Eckhart thought about this for a moment and replied, "I'm not sure if you can put this on a résumé, or I'm not even sure it can help you get a job, but the thing I am most proud of is that I don't think when I don't want to."

To me, this was an incredible statement. When you consider that most of our thought is truly "waste," this becomes a powerful practice. How much of your time is spent in worry, or fear, or concern? Think of the amount of negativity that occurs within you that you give weight to. So many variables impact us that are beyond our control, and if we let these thoughts and anxieties take hold inside of us, they will ultimately derail our internal drive and pull us away from the results we could truly be achieving with a focused forward-thinking mind-set.

Think of the amount of negativity that occurs within you that you give weight to. So many variables impact us that are beyond our control, and if we let these thoughts and anxieties take hold inside of us, they will ultimately derail our internal drive and pull us away from the results we could truly be achieving with a focused forward-thinking mind-set.

Balance

It's vitally important that you invest time in all three areas of: career, family, and health. To find your ultimate success in life, you will feel well balanced in all three dimensions and create a level of satisfaction that is rare in this world. Once you do accomplish balance in all three dimensions, the level of calm and focus and satisfaction you will experience is unparalleled.

Epilogue

S ome time has passed since I originally wrote this book, allowing me the benefit of hindsight. Hindsight is a gift, if we chose to recognize it as such. The ability to reflect upon the past and our role in the creation of our past and the learning experiences hindsight provides can be very enlightening.

I still believe one of the most challenging things we need to do as individuals is acknowledging our role in our journey down the path of success. Understanding that you ultimately have all the control to be successful inside yourself is a heavy burden to bear. It becomes so easy to play the blame game and pull out our victim card, but in the end, it is still our actions, our thoughts, our efforts, and our execution that has landed all of us exactly where we are today.

As experiences and days and months and years pass, in the end, we find ourselves firmly in the middle of who we are as an individual, as a coworker, as a friend, and as a spouse or a

It becomes so easy to play the blame game and pull out our victim card, but in the end, it is still our actions, our thoughts, our efforts, and our execution that has landed all of us exactly where we are today.

partner. The realization that you have built the foundation that you presently stand on can be very empowering or upsetting at the same time.

You've been given the opportunity to live a life well lived, so make sure you take the steps to make that happen in all facets of your life. When you look back and see yourself blessed with options to pursue your passions, and create the lifestyle and relationships that you truly care about, I think you will find yourself smiling in your own self-reflection. Stay true to yourself, have great integrity, and work with passion and purpose. Your own personal journey to accomplish your chosen level of success will not be easy, but it will be blessed if you truly carry yourself in this manner.

Inside of you, you need to find the realization that you can write your own script in life. You truly can write your own storybook ending if you passionately pursue your goals and understand what that path looks and feels like along your life journey. Understand that hard work and exceptional effort are all part of the path to your own success, but you can change that path at any time.

Do your best to realize that you never truly are at an impasse. Impasses in your career, your health, and your family are speed bumps in the path along life's journey. Don't let the speed bumps become the all of you. Accept them for what they are, and that is simply an obstacle. Life's challenges are part of our growth, and let's be real about it, challenges and obstacles are omnipresent. There is no escaping adversity in life.

Believe in yourself, and take action on that belief. Appreciate the people you love and care about, and take care of your own physical health. Live a passionate life, and work well, love well, and live well. Each person's path to success is their own, but in the end, we all are pursuing a sense of accomplishment, a sense of matter to the world we deem close to us, and more smiles than tears.

Live a passionate life, and work well, love well, and live well.

Live your life well, and listen to the inner voices of belief and success inside of you. After all, being true to yourself and following the passion your inner self directs you to follow is what makes your life's journey worth living. With passion and purpose, and being true to yourself, you can always become the game changer in your own life to create the storybook ending we all yearn for.

About the Author

Kyle Dietrich has 25+ years of experience in sales and marketing, sales leadership, operations management, and leadership development. He has operated and produced exceptional results individually, and via his teams in some of the best of financial times and in some of the worst financial times in recent history. Through his experiences in the very competitive finance sector, he has built a winning recipe for success that has been applied in practice. Meaning Kyle does not operate in theory, he has been in the trenches in some of the most competitive intensive industries, and found ways to build high achievers through a consistent process involving personal accountability, and defined execution that consistently garners results at a very high level.

Kyle resides in the Los Angeles area, near the beautiful CA coastline with his fiancé' and teenage son. He continues to successfully operate as a Sr. Executive in the business world with a multibillion dollar company, while writing and speaking in his spare time.

www.ingramcontent.com/pod-product-compliance
Lightning Source LLC
Chambersburg PA
CBHW061022220326
41597CB00017BB/2321